FUNFAX™

PREHISTORIC BEASTS

Written by Martin Noble

ACKNOWLEDGEMENTS

The publisher would like to thank the following for
their kind permission to reproduce the photographs:

MUSEUM SOURCES:

Natural History Museum, London

Royal Tyrrell Museum of
Palaeontology, Alberta, USA

Naturmuseum Senckenberg,
Frankfurt, Germany

American Museum of Natural
History, New York, NY, USA

MODELS:

Jeremy Hunt
Roby Braun
John Holmes
Centaur Studios

ILLUSTRATIONS:

Giuliano Fornari
Steve Kirk

ADDITIONAL PHOTOGRAPHY:

Colin Keates
Dave King
Lynton Gardiner
Andy Crawford
Harry Taylor
Matthew Ward
Jane Burton
Dave Rudkin
John Downs
Steve Gorton
Lynton Gardiner

FUNFAX™

A Funfax Book
First published in Great Britain by Funfax Ltd.,
an imprint of Dorling Kindersley Limited,
9 Henrietta Street, London WC2E 8PS

KU-214-363

MEET THE DINOSAURS

From around 248 to 65 million years ago, dinosaurs roamed the Earth. They were a group of reptiles (cold-blooded animals with a backbone) that laid eggs and had scaly skin. They were first called dinosaurs in 1841 by Dr Richard Owen. The word is Greek and means 'terrible lizard'.

The earliest dinosaurs had deadly, slashing teeth and claws which they used to kill and eat other reptiles. These were the carnivores, and they liked meat.

Different Diets

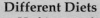

Herbivores, plant-eating dinosaurs, evolved (developed) from carnivores and became their prey. Omnivores were dinosaurs which were both meat-eating and plant-eating.

*Apatosaurus –
a herbivore*

Triassic Dinosaurs

The Age of Dinosaurs began in the Triassic Period (around 248-208 million years ago). The first known dinosaurs evolved from pre-dinosaur reptiles. From the early predatory dinosaurs evolved plant-eaters. From the small bipedal (two-legged) plant-eaters, emerged four-legged creatures as big as buses.

Iguanodon – a Cretaceous herbivore

Jurassic Dinosaurs

During the Jurassic Period (208-144 million years ago), new, enormous dinosaurs emerged. Herbivores became the prey of megalosaurids, allosaurids and other huge, sharp-fanged predators.

Cretaceous Dinosaurs

During the Cretaceous Period (144-65 million years ago), toothless, bird-like dinosaurs emerged. Tyrannosaurids, the heaviest land predators, now had to compete against new and powerful plant-eaters. At the end of this age, dinosaurs became extinct (they died out).

FIRST OF THE MEAT-EATERS

The earliest-known dinosaurs were the carnivorous (flesh-eating) herrerasaurids, such as Herrerasaurus and Staurikosaurus.

'Herrera's Lizard'

Herrerasaurus was a two-legged flesh-eater. Measuring around 3 m (10 ft) long, it had sharp teeth, short, bird-like, folding arms, long, agile legs and four-toed feet. The group herrerasauria may have given rise to all other dinosaurs. Fossils have been found in Argentina.

'Southern Cross Lizard'

Staurikosaurus was another primitive dinosaur. A speedy, lightly built, two-legged carnivore measuring 2 m (6 ft 6 in) long and weighing around 30 kg (66 lb), this dinosaur had a large head, sharp teeth, short arms, long legs and a long tail, five toes and fingers, and only two vertebrae (backbones) joining the spine to the hips.

Staurikosaurus

What Was Their Prey?

Life on Earth was originally water-based until amphibians, living on land and in water, evolved from meat-eating fish. Only after reptiles conquered the land did vertebrates (those creatures with a backbone) begin eating plants...and meat-eating dinosaurs were there already, waiting to snap them up!

Reptile Eats Reptile

During the Triassic Period, many sprawling reptiles and amphibians were replaced by a group of reptiles called thecodonts. Thecodonts then died out, being killed by the earliest dinosaurs such as Herrerasaurus and Staurikosaurus.

Thecodonts

Dinosaur Eats Dinosaur

Small predators chased lizards, seizing them in sharp-clawed hands, then swallowed them headfirst. Others roamed in packs, creeping up on big plant-eaters then killing them with a sudden rush. Dinosaurs ate each other, theropods striking with their fangs, and sharp claws on their toes and fingers. The toothless varieties made do with insects, or dug up and ate other dinosaurs' eggs.

The first plant-eaters appeared during the late Triassic Period, and the first large group was the prosauropods. These dinosaurs lived throughout the world, until early Jurassic times.

Typical Features

Typical prosauropod features included a small head containing leaf-shaped teeth, a relatively long neck and tail, and hind limbs that were longer than the front limbs. All known prosauropods had large, curved thumb-claws.

Anchisaurus ('near lizard') was one of the smaller prosauropods – around 2.1 m (7 ft) long and weighing approximately 27 kg (60 lb). It had a small, slim-snouted head with ridged teeth for shredding leaves. It probably walked on all fours, but could have reared up on its back legs to feed.

Anchisaurus

How Big?

Melanorosaurus ('black mountain lizard') was one of the largest prosauropods, measuring around 12.2 m (40 ft) long – that's about as long as a bus!

Bigger and Bigger

Small, early bipedal prosauropods probably gave rise to huge, bulky quadrupedal (four-legged) varieties during the Triassic Period. By the end of Jurassic times, dinosaurs had evolved into the colossal sauropods. (Find out more on page 8.)

'Different Teeth Lizard'

Heterodontosaurus was an early dinosaur – a small, fast plant-eater measuring around 1.2 m (3ft 11 in) long. It had short, curved tusks (possibly only in males), small, sharp cutting teeth, and closely-packed, grinding cheek teeth.

Heterodontosaurus

Sauropods were the largest land animals ever. They were plant-eaters which lived all over the world from the Jurassic Period until the end of the Cretaceous Period.

Prehistoric Giraffes

Sauropods had pillar-like legs to support a body that was perhaps bigger than several elephants. Their five-toed feet had a large, fleshy heel. Sauropods had very long necks – resembling modern-day giraffes – and had long tails to match. Their heads were very small compared to their bodies

Non-Stop Guzzler

As plant-eaters, sauropods probably spent lots of time eating to fuel their enormous bodies. They defended themselves against predators by using their whip-like tails and large, stamping feet.

Barosaurus

Inside a Sauropod's Belly

Sauropods couldn't chew their food because their teeth were the wrong shape. Instead, they deliberately swallowed stones which we call gastroliths (stomach stones). Gastroliths were used to grind up food after it was swallowed.

Brachiosaurus

Ancient Footprints

Brachiosaurus, Diplodocus, Apatosaurus and Mamenchisaurus were all sauropods. For a long time, experts believed that sauropods were so big and heavy that they could only have lived in water, because it supported their weight. However, when fossilised Apatosaurus footprints from ancient shores were discovered, they changed their minds.

A RECORD NECK

Mamenchisaurus had a neck that was three times the size of a giraffe's. In comparison to this neck, its head was tiny. This huge dinosaur was perfectly designed for its lifestyle. It could easily feed from the tops of the tallest trees where few others could reach.

Mamenchisaurus

Vacuuming, Jurassic Style

Mamenchisaurus' neck had a record 19 vertebrae. It was strong and flexible, capable of raising and lowering with ease, similar to a modern-day construction crane. Its head was lightweight and compact, allowing the dinosaur to manoeuvre itself through leafy branches.

Mamenchisaurus may also have eaten plants from shallow lakes, swinging its neck from side to side, like a powerful vacuum hose. This dinosaur's body was designed to support its enormous weight. Its backbones were strong, yet hollow for lightness, and muscular legs acted like pillars.

Family Ties

Mamenchisaurus was possibly 27 m (89 ft) long, and had the longest neck – measuring up to 15 m (49 ft)! It belonged to the euhelopodid family of sauropods, and lived in the late Jurassic Period. Euhelopodids were large, four-legged plant-eaters, and have only been found in China. Like Mamenchisaurus, many euhelopodids had amazingly long necks.

Evidence

Mamenchisaurus remains have been found in Sichuan, Gansu and Xingjiang, China.

Mamenchisaurus skeleton

Close Relatives

Euhelopus – measured around 10-15 m (33-50ft) long.

Omeisaurus – measured around 20 m (66 ft) long.

Tienshanosauraus – measured around 12 m (40 ft) long.

Long Neck, Long Tail

Another massive, long-necked sauropod was Diplodocus. This dinosaur measured around 26 m (86 ft) long. Like Mamenchisaurus, it had a long neck, and it also had a long tail.

MUNCHING ON PLANTS

Eating a diet of plants causes animals more problems than eating meat. Plants are made of tough materials such as cellulose, and these need to be broken down before digestion can take place in the animal's stomach. Life was no picnic for prehistoric plant-eaters. They coped with their diet in a variety of ways.

Powerful Jaws and Teeth

Dinosaurs such as Triceratops ate tough, fibrous plants. Triceratops, like many ceratopsians (see pages 16-17), had extremely powerful jaws. After tearing off the vegetation with its beak, it would then have sliced up the food using its sharp, scissor-like teeth.

Triceratops skull

No Chewing!

Sauropods' teeth were either spoon-shaped for nipping, or peg-shaped for raking in leaves.but they couldn't chew! Gastroliths had to do the work of grinding up the food, which could also have been fermented by bacteria, as in a cow's stomach.

Spoon-shaped sauropod tooth

Chopped Before Swallowing

Hadrosaurs had lots of teeth for chopping and grinding food; Edmontosaurus had around 1,000 strong teeth in its cheek region. These dinosaurs could also store extra food in their cheeks, like hamsters.

Small Teeth

The armoured ankylosaurs such as Sauropelta had small teeth which were only good for eating soft plants. No dinosaur had flat teeth like our molars, which we use to crush and grind our food.

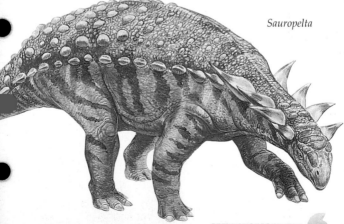

Sauropelta

Plant-eating Stegosaurus was the first plate-backed dinosaur ever found. The triangular plates jutting out of its back made it look bigger than it really was – useful for scaring off enemies. They may also have worked like solar panels, trapping the Sun's heat and transferring it to the body.

Stegosaurus

Golf Ball-Sized Brain

Stegosaurus' head was only 40 cm (16 in) long. It was narrow, with a rounded beak like that of a turtle. Stegosaurus had a very small brain in relation to its large body. It was around the size of a golf ball, weighing 78 g (2.5 oz).

Sting in the Tail

Stegosaurus' tail was thick and heavy, with four tall spines at its base; these were effective weapons against predators.

When and Where it Lived

Stegosaurus lived in the late Jurassic Period, in what is now the United States of America. Remains have been found in Colorado, Oklahoma, Utah and Wyoming. It was named in 1877, after an incomplete skeleton was discovered in Colorado.

Stegosaurus' Foes

Allosaurus ('different lizard') was one predator that may have fallen foul of Stegosaurus' spikes. This large flesh-eater measured around 11 m (36 ft) long and was the most abundant predator in late Jurassic North America.

Family Ties

Stegosaurus belonged to the stegosaur family, a group of dinosaurs that lived from the Jurassic to the Cretaceous Period, in what are now North America, Europe, Africa and Asia. Stegosaurs were generally medium-sized dinosaurs, with bulky bodies that weighed up to 1.5 tonnes.

Other Stegosaurs

There were two main subgroups (smaller groups) of stegosaurs: stegosaurids, such as Stegosaurus, Tuojiangosaurus and Kentrosaurus, and the huayangosaurids. Huayangosaurus was the only known huayangosaurid.

Biggest of the Breed

Stegosaurus was certainly the biggest stegosaur, measuring up to 9 m (30 ft) – that's three times the average size of a stegosaur.

Ceratopsians were a group of herbivorous dinosaurs that walked on four legs and had a parrot-like beak; they flourished during the Cretaceous Period.

Ceratopsians were divided into three subgroups: protoceratopsids, ceratopsids and psittacosaurids. Some of this group had distinctive features which acted as protection against ferocious meat-eaters such as Tyrannosaurus rex.

Frightening Frill

Protoceratopsids, such as Protoceratops, Bagaceratops and Microceratops, were relatively small, ranging from 76 cm (30 in) to 3 m (10 ft) long. They had a small, bony frill over the neck, and experts believe this may have been used for various purposes: to frighten predators, to protect the neck, to attract mates or to anchor the jaw muscles. Some also had brow ridges and small horns on their noses and cheeks.

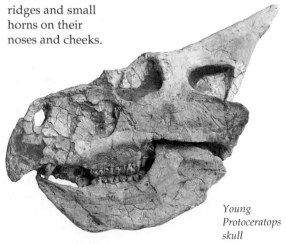

Young Protoceratops skull

Ceratopsids –Show-Offs!

Ceratopsids, such as Torosaurus ('bull lizard') and Triceratops ('three-horned face'), had large neck frills, and horns on their brow and nose. The brow horns measured up to 1.5 m (5 ft) long.

Ceratopsids had huge heads; they also had bulky bodies, pillar-like limbs and hoof like claws. They roamed in herds, browsed on low-growing vegetation and probably charged when threatened.

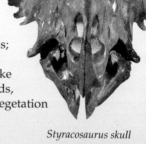

Styracosaurus skull

Horns on the Cheek

Psittacosaurus was a fairly small dinosaur, measuring around 2 m (6 ft 6 in) long. It had the parrot-like ceratopsian beak, but it did not have a bony neck frill. This dinosaur had long back legs and strong, short front limbs, complete with blunt claws suitable for walking on or grasping leaves. Its long tail counter-balanced the front part of its body. Fossil remains of Psittacosaurus have been found in Mongolia, Siberia and Europe.

Psittacosaurus skull

Tyrannosaurus rex ('tyrant lizard') is the biggest meat-eating land animal ever to have lived. It had an enormous head, a barrel-shaped body, and walked upright on long, powerful hind legs and three-taloned feet. It had tiny, two-clawed hands. Standing, it would have been tall enough to peek into a second-storey window.

Family Ties

Tyrannosaurus rex belonged to the tyrannosaurids, a close-knit group of late Cretaceous theropods. (Theropods walked on two legs and were meat-eaters.) Three known relatives are Daspletosaurus, Tarbosaurus – both similar types – and Albertosaurus, which was more lightly built.

How Big Was Big?

At a length of 14 m (46 ft) and a height of 5.6 m (18 ft 6 in), T. rex was substantially bigger than its relative, Daspletosaurus, whose length was 9 m (29 ft 6 in). Weighing around 6 tonnes, T. rex is thought to have been able to run at speeds of between 24 to 40 kph (15 to 25 mph).

Terrible Teeth

T. rex had a massive skull, with powerful jaws that held its vicious teeth. These serrated teeth measured around 18 cm (7 in).

Where and When it Lived

T. rex remains have been found in Colorado, Montana, New Mexico, South Dakota, Wyoming, China and Mongolia. It is one of the last known dinosaurs, living on Earth around 70-65 million years ago, during the Cretaceous Period.

Up or Down?

For many years after its discovery, Tyrannosaurus rex was incorrectly displayed with its long tail dragging on the ground. It is now thought that the tail stuck out, balanced in the air.

Strong Skeleton

Because of its massive size, T. rex needed a skeleton which was strong enough to support its bulk, yet light enough to allow it to run after prey. Its massive skull, built to withstand the impact from crashing into victims, was supported by a stout neck, and the backbones acted like a massive girder.

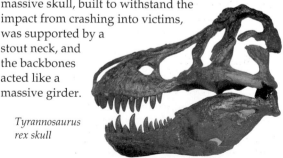

Tyrannosaurus rex skull

T. rex was a ferocious hunter. Following and ambushing herds of plant-eaters, it judged distances with its forward-facing eyes. Moving in for the kill, tail swinging, it lunged forward with its massive jaws open, ramming mouth first into its prey.

Just One Bite

T. rex could kill with one crushing bite of its steak-knife teeth. After clamping its teeth around the victim, it twisted its powerful neck to rip away flesh. It probably pinned down the carcass with its large, bird-like feet. T. rex had a huge appetite and could easily have eaten its own weight in meat every week. As well as hunting, it probably stole the kills of other animals to survive. Tyrannosaurus skeletons have shown broken bones, which experts believe were sustained in numerous fights.

Laid-Back Lifestyle

Unlike T. rex, Albertosaurus is thought by some experts to have been sluggish and slow moving. It may have laid on the ground until it was hungry, then wandered off to search for food, possibly the carcasses of dead animals. Other experts think it may have been an active hunter with even more stamina than T. rex.

On the Move

In spite of its great weight, T. rex was not a slow, lumbering creature. Like today's rhinoceros, which has pillar-like legs to support its weight, T. rex could run fast, but only over short distances. It is hard to imagine a six-tonne tyrannosaurid chasing a plant-eater for several kilometres. It probably ambushed its prey, catching it after a short chase.

Sometimes, even mighty T. rex met its match. Triceratops was well-protected against this vicious predator.

Triceratops' giant, bony frill made its head look huge and frightening, to deter prowling carnivores. The long, sharp horns on its forehead and the snout added to the threatening appearance. This dinosaur even had specially strengthened bones in its neck and hip areas, and on the roof of its skull, to withstand great shocks if it charged into an attacker.

The Monster Attacks
Just imagine the scene: a hungry T. rex spots a Triceratops, feeding away from its herd. The meat-eater rushes at its prey, intending to kill the lone plant-eater with one fatal bite from its dagger-like teeth.

Triceratops Charges

Triceratops stands its ground, preparing to charge
at the ferocious enemy. It shakes its head and
lunges towards its attacker, bellowing as it charges.
It runs perhaps as fast as 25 kph (over 15 mph),
and tries to stab Tyrannosaurus' belly with
its horns. If it succeeds, it may escape
death – this time.

A Cloud of Dust

Pawing the ground, its legs kicking up a cloud of
dust to confuse its attacker, Triceratops hisses at
T. rex, looking for a way to escape the hunter's
razor-sharp, slashing teeth. But Tyrannosaurus is
growing tired and decides to give up the fight and
hunt a weaker animal.

Another worthy foe of T. rex was Euoplocephalus ('well-armoured head') of the ankylosaur family – a four-legged, armoured dinosaur, measuring up to 7 m (23 ft) long and weighing around 2 tonnes.

This dinosaur had a broad-beaked head and massive limbs. Like many other plated dinosaurs, it had leathery skin studded with bony lumps and bumps. Its spiked, bony tail club was a dangerous weapon.

Euoplocephalus

Stegosaurus also had a tail that acted as a useful piece of defence equipment; it was tipped with four tall spines. When attacked, the dinosaur could have swung this tail using powerful muscles, hoping to lodge the spines in its enemy's flesh.

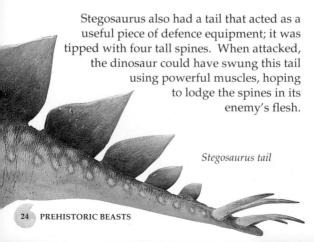

Stegosaurus tail

Spiky, Armoured Plant-Eater

Edmontonia, of the nodosaurid family, was
well-equipped to defend itself against T. rex.
A large, four-legged plant-eater, this dinosaur
measured 7 m (23 ft) long and had tough bony
plates and fierce spikes.

Edmontonia

'Thick-Headed Lizard'

Pachycephalosaurus was one of the bone-headed
dinosaurs. It had a high-domed braincase, a low,
spiky snout and sharp knobs at the back of the
head, making it look like a crash helmet. It would
have used this 'crash helmet' to defend itself
against predators such as Albertosaurus.

SAFETY IN NUMBERS?

What better way to keep away hungry predators than to travel around in herds. Hadrosaurs were herd dinosaurs. They were some of the last dinosaurs alive, appearing around 100 million years ago. They lived in eastern Asia, western North America and southern South America. It is thought that they may have swam between these different lands and stopped off at islands along the way.

Hadrosaurs are also known as 'duckbills' because of their wide, flat, toothless beaks which were used to snip off vegetation.

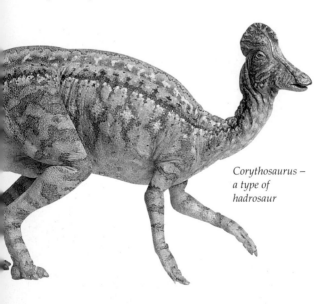

Corythosaurus – a type of hadrosaur

Crested Hadrosaur

Parasaurolophus was a huge hadrosaur – around 10 m (33 ft) long and over 2 tonnes in weight. It had a long, curved tube that arched back from its head and was around 1.5 m (5 ft) long. This was filled with air passages which may have emitted low-frequency sounds, possibly for communicating with other dinosaurs.

All-Round Athlete

Parasaurolophus had remarkable vision and acute hearing. While browsing in herds, these keen senses kept the dinosaur alert to approaching danger. It could run and was possibly able to swim, too.

All Beak and Teeth

Parasaurolophus probably ate tough tree material such as pine needles and oak leaves. Behind its beak were several rows of teeth, used for crushing and grinding. Some hadrosaurs had more than 300 in each jaw.

Parasaurolophus skull

Evidence

Remains have been found in Alberta, New Mexico and Utah.

KEEPING ORDER

Measuring around 8 m (26 ft) long, Pachycephalosaurus was the largest dinosaur in a group known as 'boneheads' Its skull had a very thick, bony top which had bumps at the front and back. At around 25 cm (10 in) thick, the skull protected the animal's brain during head-butting contests.

Head to Head
Like modern-day male goats, Pachycephalosaurus' probably butted one another to fight for mates and to keep order in the herd.

Pachycephalosaurus skull

Family Ties
Pachycephalosaurus belonged to the pachycephalosaur family, a relatively rare and puzzling group of plant-eating dinosaurs which lived towards the end of the Cretaceous Period.

Fossil Discoveries
In the late 19th century, a single pachycephalosaur tooth was found in the Judith River Beds of Montana. It wasn't until 1940, when an almost complete skull of another thick-headed dinosaur was discovered, that the name Pachycephalosaurus was finally given.

Evidence

As well as being discovered in North America, pachycephalosaur remains have also been found in Madagascar, China and Mongolia.

Two Groups

Pachycephalosaurs have been divided into two forms: high-domed pachycephalosaurids, such as Pachycephalosaurus, and low-domed homalocephalids, such as Homalocephale. Homalocephalids had a flat, fairly smooth skull roof with nodes along the back. The difference in the animals' head shapes was probably to do with their separate behaviour patterns. Pachycephalosaurids probably used their high domes to butt opponents, while homalocephalids might have used their lower domes to push against opponents' skulls.

Lifestyle

Pachycephalosaurids probably lived in small groups in upland areas. They ate leaves, fruits, seeds and perhaps insects. They were not designed for running fast to escape danger, but could probably detect it with their sharp eyes and a keen sense of smell. If attacked, they might have charged, head down.

Oak leaves

Compsognathus is one of the smallest dinosaurs ever found. Roughly the size of a chicken, it measured up to 0.7 m (2.5ft) long and weighed around 3 kg (6.5 lbs). This little dinosaur resembled a wingless bird, with bird-like, clawed feet.

Compsognathus

Family Ties

Compsognathus ('pretty jaw') was a theropod and also a coelurosaur. Coelurosaurs were an odd mixture of small theropods, who were very alike. They were all fast runners, hunting mammals and insects. They also cleaned up carcasses.

Lizard-Eater

Compsognathus had a long neck, a narrow mouth and razor-sharp teeth. It was a clever, speedy hunter, and ate small vertebrates and insects. It probably grasped prey in its two-clawed hands.

Compsognathus sped along on two legs, using its long tail as a counterbalance. It had good senses – essential in a world full of bigger dinosaurs.

Where It Lived

Compsognathus lived during the late Jurassic Period.

It probably lived on the shores of lakes and lagoons; its footprints have been found imbedded in sand and mud. This kind of habitat was popular with these dinosaurs, as there was plenty of water, vegetation and sandy soil in which to lay their eggs.

Compsognathus

Short Life Span

This small dinosaur probably had a short life span, and may have laid large clutches of eggs to make sure that its species survived.

Perfect Specimen

Few Compsognathus specimens have been unearthed. A single complete skeleton was discovered in Germany, in 1861, and was one of the most completely preserved sets of dinosaur bones ever found. There are probably so few remains because small dinosaurs' bones disintegrated before they could fossilise.

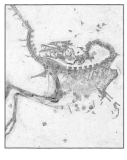

Compsognathus skeleton

Velociraptor flourished in the late Cretaceous Period. It was a fast, smart and highly-effective hunter, and well-equipped for attack. It could also have beaten a hasty retreat from larger predators. Velociraptor's design was so successful that its form hardly changed for 50 million years!

Ferocious Beast

Velociraptor walked on two feet and had hands that could grasp and clutch its victims. It was perfectly designed to capture swift, lightweight prey, but its wide jaws could deal with larger animals, too. Velociraptor's most distinguishing feature must be the sickle-like claw on each hind foot – just right for slashing meat. These claws were around 15 cm (6 in) long, and could be held out of the way when running.

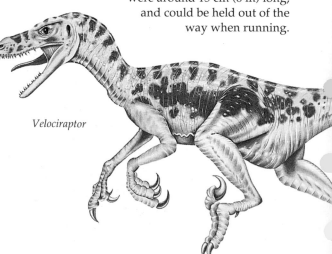

Velociraptor

Family Ties

Velociraptor belonged to the family of theropods known as dromaeosaurs. It has also been put in another group – that of the feathered, winged Archaeopteryx, believed to be a relative of the first birds. Although Velociraptors had no feathers and couldn't fly, they had a lot in common with primitive birds. Birds have unique, 'saddle-shaped' necks. This can be seen in Velociraptor, which had a lightly built, upturned skull and curved neck. The word 'raptor' itself means 'bird of prey'.

Steering Tail

Velociraptor's long, stiff, rudder-like tail helped it to steer as it zoomed along.

Locked in Combat

An amazing fossil discovery was made when two dinosaurs were found locked in battle. One was a Velociraptor, the other a ceratopsian called Protoceratops. Each dinosaur had fatally wounded the other.

Evidence

Velociraptor remains have been found in North America, China, Mongolia and Russia.

Archaeopteryx

Velociraptor killed by raking a victim's limbs or belly with its sickle-like claws, probably disembowelling the prey; both claws were used together, for maximum effect. It used its vicious jaws to bite its victim's flesh.

Pack Hunters

It is believed that Velociraptors hunted in packs. Individual animals would have picked on small lizards or mammals, but as pack animals, they could very effectively bring down much larger plant-eating dinosaurs such as Sauropelta (below).

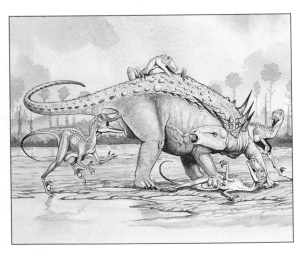

One day in Montana...

A pack of Velociraptors, numbering at least four, would have surrounded the larger dinosaur. The Velociraptors were likely to have suffered many casualties as the heavily-armoured Sauropelta used its tail to defend itself.

Tail Balance

The Velociraptors' stiffened tails acted as a counterbalance to the violent actions of the attack. As the Velociraptors slashed at Sauropelta with their retractable claws, they used their powerful, stiffened tails to balance themselves.

Two Footed

It is also thought that the Velociraptors were able to perform a powerful two-footed hop to pounce on to the victim.

No Escape

As Sauropelta desperately tried to escape, biting and kicking, its power was no match for the attackers. Still alive, Sauropelta staggered and fell as the Velociraptors start to eat it.

Evidence

And all this could actually have happened. There is a quarry in Montana, USA that includes pieces of a Sauropelta which Velociraptors may have been feeding upon when they all died together.

A SPEEDY GETAWAY

At 6 m (20 ft) long, Gallimimus ('fowl mimic') was the largest of the bird-like dinosaurs.

It was an omnivore, and may have scratched away soil to eat buried eggs. With its toothless beak and long tail, Gallimimus resembled a modern-day ostrich. It had large eyes, a small head, a long, shaped neck and powerful, long hind limbs that ended in three-toed feet. Its thin 'arms' had elbow joints.

Zooming Along

Gallimimus could have zoomed along at up to 40 kph (25 mph). When it ran, it held its tail out for balance. It may have kicked enemies, but its main defence was a speedy getaway.

Gallimimus

Family Ties

Gallimimus lived in the late Cretaceous Period. It belonged to a group of dinosaurs known as ornithomimosaurs.

Evidence
Remains have been found in southern Mongolia.

Close Relations
Dromiceiomimus and Ornithomimus were two other ornithomimosaurs. Dromiceiomimus was smaller than Gallimimus, and could run at speeds of up to 64.4 kph (40 mph). Ornithomimus measured around 3.5 m (11 ft 6 in) long and could zip along at speeds of up to 60 kph (37 mph).

What Big Eyes You Had...
Gallimimus' eyes were bigger than those of an ostrich, yet its skull was narrower. Its eyeballs were actually flattened and could not move much in their sockets. This means that Gallimimus must have had to flick its head to see around.

It's Behind You!
Because Gallimimus' eyes faced sideways, its binocular vision (the ability to use both eyes at the same time) was limited. However, Gallimimus could detect predators from behind.

Gallimimus

Advantages of a Full Belly
Gallimimus kept its belly at least partly filled with digesting plant material. This was so that micro-organisms living there could keep on breaking down plant material.

Palaeontology is the study of the geological past; basically it is the study of rocks and fossils. Scientists have created maps to show the different ages of rocks. Dinosaur fossils are found throughout the world, in rocks many millions of years old.

Fossil Creation

When most animals die, their remains are broken up and destroyed by the weather and by other animals. However, sometimes their bodies are washed into rivers or lakes and quickly covered by sand and mud; in a desert the remains might be covered by wind-blown sand. This is how some dinosaurs became preserved.

Hadrosaurus skeleton

Over millions of years, more and more sand and mud piled on top of the remains. These 'sediments' then gradually turned into sandstone, limestone and shale, and the soft parts of the dinosaurs' scaly skin lasted long enough to leave their impression in the fine mud. Fragile eggshells were also turned into fossils.

Turned to Stone

The fossils discovered by scientists are different from the dinosaurs' original remains. Here are some examples of finds.

Teeth: the hardest parts of all, often surviving with little change at all.

Moulds: sometimes bones are dissolved, leaving bone-shaped hollow spaces. This kind of fossil is called a mould.

Casts: a mould that was later filled by other minerals became a cast. Some moulds or casts can even show a dinosaur's scaly skin.

Trace fossils: other traces left by dinosaurs, including:

Ichnites: fossil footprints. They show where dinosaurs walked, whether they walked on two or four legs, how fast they moved (fast runners' footprints would be far apart), and whether they travelled on their own or in herds.

Coprolites: fossilised dinosaur droppings.

Ooliths: fossilised eggs.

Fossilised Protoceratops eggs

Dinosaur discoveries are rare; often they lie buried in layers of rock on hillsides, on beaches, or in quarries. Only once the remains are uncovered can a team of experts go to work and 'excavate' the fossilised dinosaur.

Tools of the Trade

Experts use pickaxes and shovels to clear away rock; hammers and sharp chisels are used when the work involves close contact with the bone; brushes are used to sweep away the dust. Workers wear protective goggles, and hard hats are essential for working near cliffs.

Protecting the Fossils

Wet tissue paper is spread over a fossil to protect the surface. Thick bandages or sacking are soaked in plaster and then spread over the tissue paper. When this has hardened, the fossil is carefully turned over. Its other side is also covered with paper and plaster bandage. When both sides have been plastered, the fossil can be lifted out.

Putting Dinosaurs Together Again

After the hard work of excavation, the precious fossils are taken back to a laboratory for preparation, study and display. They are removed from their protective jackets, then the remaining rock or earth is cleaned away with chisels, delicate power tools and chemicals. The cleaned bones are studied, to work out how they fitted together in real life. Tell-tale clues can be found on the bone surface – muscles sometimes leave clear marks where they were attached.

Adding the Flesh

It may take some time for scientists to work out how the bones fitted together – missing bones may have to be modelled from plaster. Skin impressions have sometimes been preserved to aid the model maker, but colour is simply a matter of guesswork.

Building a dinosaur skeleton

Tiny Hands

The arms and hands of Tyrannosaurus, as with other tyrannosaurids, were among its most bizarre features. The shoulder bones were moderately large, but the arms were minute and ended in tiny, two-clawed hands.

Handy Hands

There are various theories regarding T. rex's two-clawed hands. They were too short to reach the mouth, so they weren't used for feeding, and they couldn't have been used to walk on, either. One suggestion is that the hands might have been used to grip during mating, or to anchor the front of the body when the animal raised itself from the ground.

Tyrannosaurus rex's little arms

Parasaurolophus' Crest

There have been a number of theories about the function of Parasaurolophus' extraordinary crest...

Underwater Snorkel

At first, experts suggested that the crest allowed the dinosaur to breathe underwater while feeding on submerged plants. However, there was no hole in the tip to let air through.

Air Storage Tank

If the crest didn't act like a snorkel, perhaps it stored air, so that the dinosaur could stay submerged for long periods. The trouble is, the crest could only have stored a very small amount of air!

Smelling Device

Parasaurolophus' crest possibly allowed it an advanced sense of smell.

Signalling Device

It is likely that the crest helped the creatures signal to one another. This would have been useful for mating.

Foliage Deflector

As Parasaurolophus lived in wooded areas, it might have used its crest to crash through foliage without damaging its head.

Dinosaurs With Wings?

In 1861, fossil hunters discovered the perfectly-preserved bones of a late Jurassic creature in a German quarry. When experts inspected it closely, they found that the reptile was covered with feathers!

Fossilised Archaeopteryx

Archaeopteryx

Mystery Wishbone

The creature was 0.9 m (3 ft) long, had thin, fine-boned legs, long, delicate toes and slim jaws with short teeth. It had feathers along its arms and the long bones of its tail. It was named Archaeopteryx ('ancient feather'), and was soon found to have other bird-like features. Most surprisingly, it had a wishbone, just like those found in the collarbones of all birds. No other animal has one. For the next hundred years, experts debated the link between dinosaurs and birds.

Startling Discovery

In the 1970s, it was found that dinosaurs like Velociraptor and Compsognathus shared several similarities with Archaeopteryx and modern birds. In 1998, a chicken-sized dinosaur with downy feathers but no wings was found and named Sinosauropteryx (meaning 'eastern feather lizard'). The evidence seems to indicate that birds are directly related to dinosaurs!

Stegosaurus' Second Brain

Stegosaurus had a tiny brain. When the backbones near the dinosaur's hips were first examined, it was found that the spinal cord formed a big bulge there. Some people thought that this might have been a second brain. It is now known that this is just the place where the nerves from Stegosaurus' back legs and tail joined its spinal cord.

More About Those Plates

The arrangement of Stegosaurus' plates is another issue that experts have debated. At first, they thought that the plates formed a single, upright line along the dinosaur's back. Some experts thought that they stuck out sideways, like a protective shield. Now the plates are generally shown arranged in two alternating rows.

Stegosaurus

Europe

Dinosaur remains have been found all over Europe, but the fossilised skeletons tend to be less complete than elsewhere. The word 'dinosaur' was first coined in England in 1841, to describe the three known giant reptiles at the time: Iguanodon ('iguana tooth'), a plant-eater found in great numbers; Megalosaurus, a large, two-legged predator; and Hylaeosaurus, a four-legged, armoured plant-eater.

North America

This part of the world has been popular with dinosaur hunters since the mid-19th century. Famous finds include: Tyrannosaurus rex, Diplodocus, Parasaurolophus, Triceratops, Euoplocephalus, Stegosaurus and Apatosaurus. New dinosaur remains are still being discovered here.

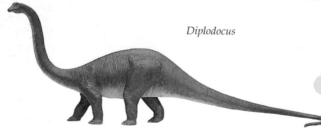

Diplodocus

South America

Much of South America is covered with dense vegetation, making it difficult to dig for dinosaur remains. However, important finds have been made in the more barren areas further south. They include plant-eating Mussaurus ('mouse lizard'), Amargasaurus and Riojasaurus, and meat-eating Herrerasaurus.

Africa

This huge continent has been home to many different kinds of dinosaurs. The oldest remains have been found in the south, while younger remains have been discovered further north. Important finds include the plant-eating Massospondylus ('massive vertebrae') and the two-legged meat-eater, Spinosaurus.

Asia

Some of the most recent and exciting finds have been made in Asia, including the plant-eaters Tuojiangosaurus, Saurolophus and Shantungosaurus, and the 'egg-thief', Oviraptor. Many dinosaur remains, including dinosaur eggs, have been discovered in the Gobi Desert.

Oviraptor

Australia

Not many dinosaur fossils have been found here. The most complete dinosaur discovered is plant-eating Muttaburrasaurus.

Antarctica

Only two dinosaurs have been excavated here so far, in the late 1980s, but there may well be many fossils under Antarctica's icy waters.

Early ideas about fossils now seem very odd: they were put there by the devil to confuse people; they were the remains of animals drowned in the flood when Noah escaped in his ark; they were mistakes that God made while creating all the animals.

Theories of Extinction

About 65 million years ago, dinosaurs, plesiosaurs, pterosaurs and many other animals of land or sea became extinct. Theories about this include dinosaurs evolved such awkward bodies that they couldn't move or breed; predatory dinosaurs ate the rest then starved; tiny mammals gobbled up dinosaur eggs. Nowadays, the most widely believed theories include drastic global change (possibly caused by a meteorite hitting Earth) or relatively slow extinction, with new creatures evolving to replace the old.